DATE DUE

Strings

Wendy Lynch

Heinemann Library
Chicago, Illinois

© 2002 Reed Educational & Professional Publishing
Published by Heinemann Library,
an imprint of Reed Educational & Professional Publishing,
Chicago, Illinois

Customer Service 888-454-2279

Visit our website at www.heinemannlibrary.com

Designed by Visual Image
Illustration by Jane Watkins
Originated by Dot Gradations
Printed and bound in South China

06 05 04 03 02
10 9 8 7 6 5 4 3 2 1

Library of Congress Cataloging-in-Publication Data
Lynch, Wendy, 1945-
 Strings / Wendy Lynch.
  p. cm. -- (Musical instruments)
 Includes bibliographical references (p.   ) and index.
 ISBN 1-58810-236-X
 1. Stringed instruments--Juvenile literature. [1. Stringed instruments.]   I. Title. II. Series.
 ML750 .L96 2001
 787'.19--dc21

                                    2001000097

Acknowledgments
The publishers would like to thank the following for permission to reproduce photographs: pp. 4, 5, 9 Pictor; pp. 6, 7, 10, 16, 17 Photodisc; p. 8 Superstock; pp. 11, 24, 28, 29 Gareth Boden; p. 13 The Stock Market; p. 14 Trevor Clifford; pp. 15, 22, 23 Robert Harding; p. 18 John Walmsley; p. 19 Jennie Woodcock/ Bubbles; p. 20 Greg Evans; p. 21 Picture Colour Library Ltd.; p. 25 Associated Press; p. 26 Ebet Roberts/ Redferns; p. 27 Steve Jennings/Retna Ltd.

Cover photograph reproduced with permission of Photodisc.

Special thanks to Susan Lerner for her comments in the preparation of this book.

Every effort has been made to contact copyright holders of any material reproduced in this book. Any omissions will be rectified in subsequent printings if notice is given to the publisher.

Some words are shown in bold, **like this.** You can find out what they mean by looking in the glossary.

Contents

Making Music Together

There are many musical instruments in the world. Each instrument makes a different sound. We can make music together by playing these instruments in an **orchestra.**

Bands and orchestras are made up of different groups of instruments. One of these groups is called the string family. You can see many stringed instruments in this orchestra.

What Are Stringed Instruments?

These are all stringed instruments. They have strings stretched over them. When the strings are played, they **vibrate** to make a sound.

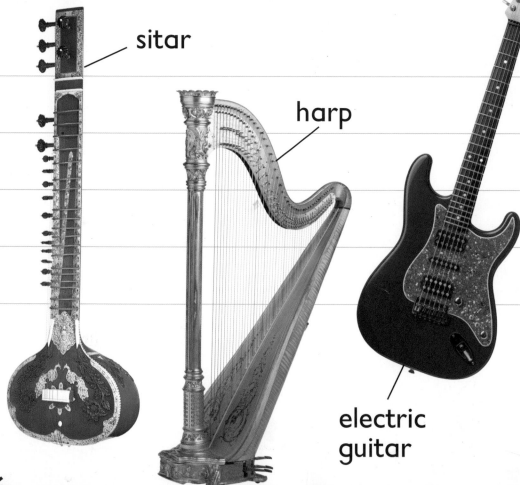

sitar

harp

electric guitar

You play some stringed instruments with a bow. This is a stick with horsehair or nylon stretched between the ends. You play others with a **plectrum,** or pick, made of wood, metal, or plastic.

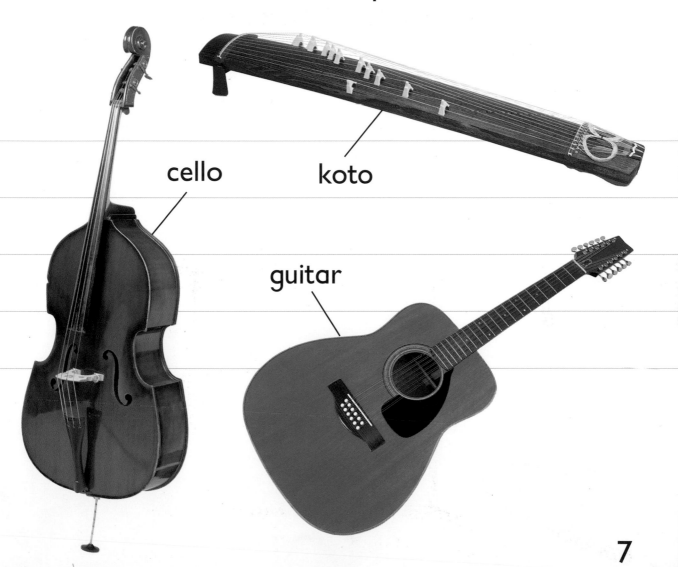

cello

koto

guitar

The Violin

The violin is a popular stringed instrument. Many children learn to play the violin when they are young. You may use a small violin at first so that your fingers can reach across the strings.

You can learn to play the violin in school or with a private teacher. When you play the violin on your own, this is called playing **solo.**

Making a Sound

The violin has four strings stretched along its **curved** body. You play it with a bow, moving the bow across the strings to make a sound.

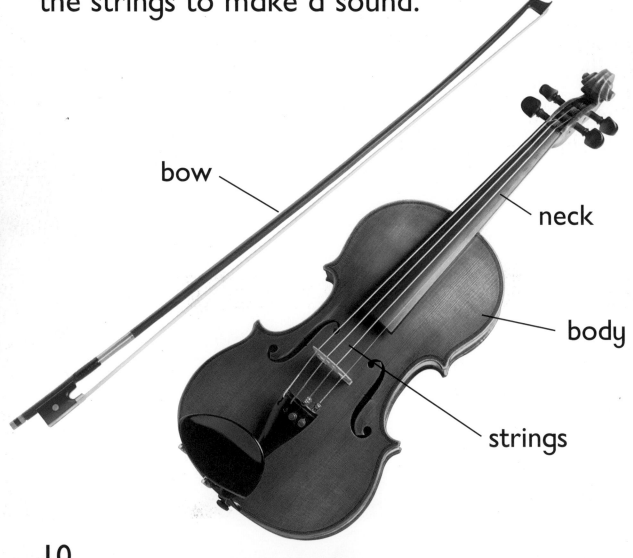

bow

neck

body

strings

The bow needs to move smoothly, without slipping. Rubbing a sticky material called **rosin** into the hairs of the bow helps it grip the strings better.

How the Sound Is Made

The body of the violin is **hollow.** It is called a sound box. When you move the bow across the strings, you make the strings **vibrate** from side to side.

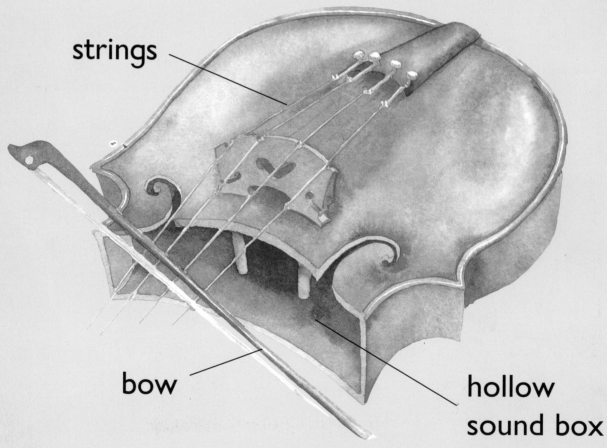

strings

bow

hollow sound box

This movement of the strings makes
the air inside the sound box vibrate.
The vibrating air makes a sound. You
can change the sound by pressing your
fingers against the strings as you play.

Types of Strings

The viola looks like the violin, but it is a bit bigger. It also has a lower **pitch,** because there is more room in its sound box for the air to **vibrate.**

violin

viola

14

The cello is much larger than the violin. It also sounds much lower. To play, you sit with the cello between your knees and move a bow across the strings.

Guitars

The guitar is a stringed instrument. You can **strum** the strings with your fingers or **pluck** them with a **plectrum.** To change the sound, you press on the strings on the guitar's neck.

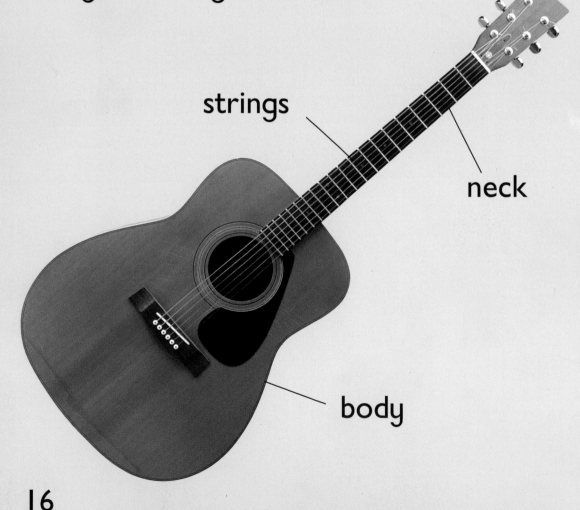

strings

neck

body

There are many different types of guitars. You can hear the steel guitar in **blues** and **folk** music. In **pop** music, you can often hear the electric and bass guitars.

electric
guitar

steel
guitar

String Concerts

You may hear stringed instruments in a concert. These instruments often play in groups. A string **quartet** includes a cello, two violins, and a viola.

Your teacher may play the guitar in school. These children are learning to sing a new song while their teacher **accompanies** them on the guitar.

The Wider Family

The harp is a **curved** instrument with 47 strings. The harpist sits and **plucks** the strings from both sides of the harp. The strings may be different colors to help the harpist find the notes.

The zither can be set on a table or held on your lap to play it. On one side of the zither are the strings that are used to play the **melody.**

Around the World

You can find stringed instruments all over the world. The sitar comes from India. It has two sets of strings, one on top of the other. You **pluck** the strings with a wire **plectrum.**

The koto is an old musical instrument
from Japan, often played by women.
A player kneels on the ground. She plucks
the strings with her thumb and first two
fingers, using an **ivory** plectrum.

Famous Musicians and Composers

Nigel Kennedy is a well-known violin player. This is a CD of him playing *The Four Seasons* by Antonio Vivaldi. Vivaldi **composed** a lot of music for the violin.

Sarah Chang began to play the violin when she was only four years old. When she was five, she played in her first concert.

String Music Today

Today, you can hear stringed instruments in **jazz, rock,** and **folk** music. The violin often plays the **melody** because its high, clear sound is pleasant and easy to hear.

A lot of today's rock and **pop** music uses electric guitars. You might also hear electric violins. The sound from these instruments comes through an **amplifier** so you can hear it better.

Sound Activity

You can make your own guitar with an empty tissue box, four rubber bands, and a pencil. Wide rubber bands make a low sound, and thin ones make a high sound. You can try some of each.

Stretch the four rubber bands over the box from end to end. These are the strings on your sound box. Place the pencil under the rubber bands next to the hole. Now **strum** your guitar!

Thinking about Strings

You can find the answers to all of these questions in this book.

1. What are two ways that stringed instruments can be played?

2. What is **rosin** used for?

3. How can you change a stringed instrument's sound?

4. Which instruments play in a string **quartet?**

5. From which country is the sitar? What is unusual about how it is made?

Glossary

accompany to play along with someone else

amplifier machine that changes electrical signals into sounds by sending them through a speaker

blues style of music that is usually slow and sad

compose to write something new

curved bent into a rounded shape

folk music traditional style of music from a place or country

ivory material from the tusk of an elephant

jazz style of music that is often made up as it is played

melody tune

orchestra large group of musicians who play their instruments together

pitch highness or lowness of a sound or musical note

plectrum small piece of wood, metal, or plastic used to pluck the strings of some stringed instruments

pluck to pull

pop popular music

quartet group of four musicians, or a piece of music written for four players

rock kind of pop music with a strong beat

rosin sticky material that comes from pine trees

solo song or piece of music for one person

strum to brush across the strings of an instrument with your fingers

vibrate to move up and down or from side to side very quickly

More Books to Read

Harris, Pamela K. *Violins*. Chanhassen, Minn.: The Child's World, Incorporated, 2000.

Kalman, Bobbie. *Musical Instruments from A to Z*. New York: Crabtree Publishing Company, 1997.

Turner, Barrie Carson. *Modern Instruments*. North Mankato, Minn.: Smart Apple Media, 2000.

Index